Where Does God Live?

AUGUST GOLD & MATTHEW J. PERLMAN

Walking Together, Finding the Way

SKYLIGHT PATHS PUBLISHING

WOODSTOCK, VERMONT

D1309382

Where Does God Live?

Library of Congress Cataloging-in-Publication Data
Gold, August, 1955–
Where does God live? / written and illustrated by August Gold and Matthew J. Perlman.
　　　　p.　　　cm.
ISBN 1-893361-39-X (pbk.)
1. God—Juvenile literature. [1. God.] I. Perlman, Matthew J., 1954–. II. Title.
BT107 .G65 2001
291.2'11—dc21

2001001924

10 9 8 7 6 5 4 3 2 1

Manufactured in Malaysia

Photos: Matthew J. Perlman. Grateful acknowledgment is given to Mark and Tricia Siegelbaum, Chelsea and Paul Smith, Christine, Bob and Ed Wall, and Diane Waller for providing additional photos.

Interior design concept: Michael Ingersoll and Greg Zukowski
Special thanks to Karen Wilder of Wilder's Word Processing, New York City.
Cover design & interior typesetting: Bridgett Taylor

SkyLight Paths, "Walking Together, Finding the Way" and colophon are trademarks of LongHill Partners, Inc., registered in the U.S. Patent and Trademark Office.

Walking Together, Finding the Way
Published by SkyLight Paths Publishing
A Division of LongHill Partners, Inc.
Sunset Farm Offices, Route 4, P.O. Box 237
Woodstock, Vermont 05091
Tel: (802) 457-4000　Fax: (802) 457-4004
www.skylightpaths.com

"Where does God live?"

was the question she had.

"God lives in us all!"
said her mom and her dad.

"God's all there is
and all that you see!"

"But I still don't see God
so how can it be?"

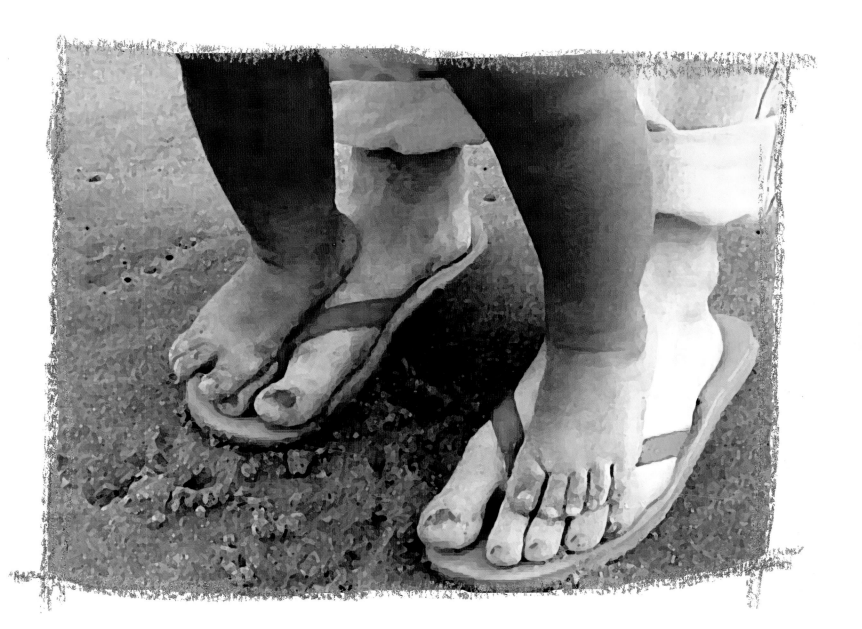

"That's 'cause you're looking
with just your eyes...
look into your heart
and you'll see God inside."

"So I'll see God
through the eyes
of my heart?!"

"Exactly," they said,
"that's just how you start!"

"You'll see
that God lives
in things
big...

and things small...

You'll find God is
everywhere—

the ALL in all.

God lives in the sun
and the black sky of night,

God lives in the **dark,**
God lives in the light.

God lives in the flowers,

the oceans
and streams,

God lives in the treetops...

God lives in your dreams.

God lives in everyone
here on the earth;
That's why we all shine
from the day of our birth.

God lives in all people,
we all are God's light;
God lives in our laughter,
God is our delight.

God lives in your wings
when you fly through the air...

God lives in your tears when
you're sad or you're scared.

God lives in your strength
when you try something new...

You're always with God
and God's always with you.

God lives with you whether
you're near or you're far;

God lives with you always
wherever you are.

And remember whatever
you say or you do,

God lives in your heart
and will always love you."

"So the God in my heart
has so much to give
that **wherever** I look
I can see where God lives!"

Now her question was answered.
She smiled. She could see:

Wherever she looked
is where God would be.

To Sofie Wall,
who with a mouth filled
with French fries asked the question
that started us all thinking:
"Where is God?"

—A.G.

To Kate and Maggie,
who answer the question for me every day.

—M.J.P.